EXPLORING CIVIL

THE BEGINNINGS

1951

SELENE CASTROVILLA

Franklin Watts®
An imprint of Scholastic Inc.

Content Consultant

A special thank you to Ryan M. Jones at the National Civil Rights Museum for his expert consultation.

Library of Congress Cataloging-in-Publication Data
Names: Castrovilla, Selene, 1966- author.
Title: The beginnings : 1951 / by Selene Castrovilla.
Other titles: Exploring civil rights.
Description: New York : Franklin Watts, an imprint of Scholastic Inc.,
   2022. | Series: Exploring civil rights | Includes bibliographical
   references and index. | Audience: Ages 10–14 | Audience: Grades 7–9 |
   Summary: "Series continuation. Narrative nonfiction, key events of the
   Civil Rights Movement in the years spanning from 1939–1954. Photographs
   throughout"— Provided by publisher.
Identifiers: LCCN 2022002605 (print) | LCCN 2022002606 (ebook) |
   ISBN 9781338800623 (library binding) | ISBN 9781338800630 (paperback) |
   ISBN 9781338800647 (ebk)
Subjects: LCSH: African Americans—Civil rights—History—Juvenile
   literature. | Civil rights movements—United States—History—20th
   century—Juvenile literature. | Civil rights workers—United
   States—Juvenile literature. | BISAC: JUVENILE NONFICTION / History /
   United States / General | JUVENILE NONFICTION / History / United States
   / 20th Century
Classification: LCC E185.61 .C293 2022 (print) | LCC E185.61 (ebook) |
   DDC 323.1196/073—dc23/eng/20220131
LC record available at https://lccn.loc.gov/2022002605
LC ebook record available at https://lccn.loc.gov/2022002606

10 9 8 7 6 5 4 3 2 1   23 24 25 26 27

Printed in China   62
First edition, 2023

Composition by Kay Petronio

COVER & TITLE PAGE:
Middleweight Champion Sugar Ray Robinson trains during his 1951 European tour.

The Topeka, Kansas, civil rights lawsuit *Brown v. Board of Education*, page 52.

Table of Contents

INTRODUCTION
The Way It Was 4

1 Black Citizens Take Action 8

2 A Look Inside 22

3 A Teenage Crusader 32

4 A Measure of How Far 42

5 A Long Journey 54

6 More Injustice 62

CONCLUSION
The Legacy of 1951 in Civil Rights History 76

Biography MAYA ANGELOU 82
Timeline 88
Glossary 90
Bibliography 92
Index 94
About the Author 96

James Nabrit, Jr., page 29.

Under Jim Crow laws, Black men and boys are imprisoned for minor violations of unfair laws.

The Way It Was

In the period directly following the American Civil War (1861–1865), three **amendments** to the U.S. Constitution sought to grant African Americans the rights they'd been denied during slavery. In 1865, the Thirteenth Amendment abolished slavery. In 1868, the Fourteenth Amendment granted **citizenship** to African Americans. And in 1870, the Fifteenth Amendment gave African American men the right to vote.

Despite those triumphs, this period also saw the introduction of Black codes, or laws passed to limit the rights and freedoms of Black Americans. They soon became known as **Jim Crow** laws, and they were especially strict in the American South. Jim Crow laws controlled where people of color could live and work.

Jim Crow laws enforced **segregation**. Under the racial policy of "separate but equal," Black Americans could be given separate facilities if the quality was equal to the white facilities. In reality, however, there was no equality. African Americans were forced to attend separate and inadequate schools, live in run-down neighborhoods, and even drink from rusty or broken public water fountains.

In 1896, a group of **activists** tried to overturn the Jim Crow laws with the Supreme Court case *Plessy v. Ferguson*. Unfortunately, when the case was lost, Jim Crow laws became even more acceptable across the country, but remained most common in the southern United States.

The Fight Begins

As Jim Crow expanded, two prominent **civil rights** organizations emerged. The National Association of Colored Women's Clubs (NACWC) was founded in 1896 by a group of politically active women, including Harriet Tubman. Members of the association dedicated themselves to fighting for voting rights and for ending racial violence in the form of **lynchings** against African Americans. In addition to lynchings, African Americans suffered severe harassment, beatings, and even bomb-ings at the hands of racist organizations like the **Ku Klux Klan** (KKK), which had millions of members by the 1920s.

The National Association for the Advancement of Colored People (NAACP), founded in 1909, followed in the NACWC's footsteps. The NAACP focused on opposing segregation and Jim Crow policies. Both organizations would be crucial in the coming fight for justice.

1951

At the start of 1951, the civil rights movement was changing into a Christian, youth, and legal effort. It would prove to be an important year in the way the Black community looked at segregated education in public schools. Local NAACP leaders and other activists spearheaded plans to end the rule of "separate but equal" and changed their strategy to achieving **integration**. Barbara Johns would organize a student strike against the miserable conditions of her Black high school. Justice for African Americans would be the other critical issue addressed by the NAACP. On Christmas night, a shocking act of violence would be committed against Harry T. Moore, the executive director of the Florida NAACP, and his wife, Harriette, leaving the Black community devastated but also determined to reach their dream of equality. ◼

Harriette and Harry Moore in Florida in the late 1940s.

Nine-year-old Linda Brown (front, right) with her classmates at the racially segregated Monroe Elementary School, in Topeka, Kansas.

1

Black Citizens Take Action

On February 28, 1951, three NAACP lawyers filed a **federal** lawsuit on behalf of thirteen Topeka, Kansas, Black parents who had tried and failed to enroll their young children in the elementary schools closest to their homes. Children who were white, Hispanic, Native American, and Asian were allowed to attend these schools. Black parents had to explain to their children that because of the color of their skin, they could not attend classes with their friends from the neighborhood. They would have to walk several blocks to a bus stop—often past the local white school—and then ride a bus to a Black school miles away.

The Black schools seemed equal in appearance and teacher salaries, but some programs were not offered, and some textbooks were not available. The bigger insult, though, was that there were only four elementary schools for Black children as compared to 18 for white children. This made attending schools in their own neighborhoods even more unlikely for African American children, and it also caused overcrowding in the all-Black schools.

On their own, Black parents felt helpless. This is where the NAACP stepped in.

Strategy

Lawsuits were a strategy of the NAACP to strike down "separate but equal" education. Black communities were at the forefront of civil rights activism, and the NAACP believed Kansas was a good place to create change. When Kansas joined the country as the 34th state back in 1861, it forbade the enslavement of African Americans. Missouri, its neighbor and the 24th state, had been permitting enslavement

Antislavery Kansas was attacked so much by its pro-slavery neighboring state Missouri during the Civil War that it became known as "Bleeding Kansas."

for 40 years. Missouri felt that its way of life was threatened by Kansas protecting its Black citizens, and it made repeated attacks on Kansas. The violence became so great that a newspaper columnist called the new state "Bleeding Kansas." But Kansas would not back down. The fact that Kansas had taken this stand against enslavement at the start of their statehood surely meant **desegregation** could be achieved there, NAACP officials reasoned.

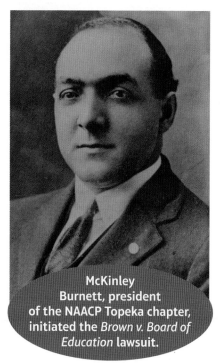

McKinley Burnett, president of the NAACP Topeka chapter, initiated the *Brown v. Board of Education* lawsuit.

They were right—to a degree.

First Class City

The NAACP succeeded in desegregating schools in smaller Kansas cities through court challenges. But in 1951, "first class cities" (with populations greater than 10,000) were still permitted to have segregated elementary schools. Topeka, the capital of Kansas, had approximately 80,000 residents at the time. Roughly 8 percent of the population was Black.

This continued segregation weighed heavily on McKinley Burnett. In 1948, he had been elected president of the NAACP's Topeka chapter. As an African American, Burnett experienced **discrimination** from childhood on and tried to end segregation. He wrote letters to government officials but never heard back. He decided to head the Topeka NAACP specifically so Black children would be given the respect and proper educational opportunities that they deserved.

Secondary Education

Topeka junior and senior high schools were integrated, but African American students in these upper grades still experienced racism. Kenneth McFarland, superintendent of schools, who was white, and Harrison Caldwell, assistant superintendent of Black schools, who was African American, did not treat the

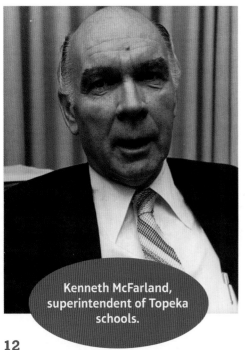

Kenneth McFarland, superintendent of Topeka schools.

Black students fairly. For example, all high school seniors were invited to a dance, but Caldwell told the manager of the establishment to prevent the Black students from entering. The white students stopped the dance in protest, but the Black students were not allowed in.

Top of the Charts

The top song of 1951 was "Too Young," sung by Black artist Nat King Cole. Released February 6, it remained number one on the Billboard chart for five weeks, and on the Best Seller chart for 29 weeks.

Cole began as a professional pianist and singer at age 15. He formed the Nat King Cole Trio with Wesley Prince on string bass and Oscar Moore on guitar. The Nat King Cole Trio gained worldwide fame, and its unique style of swing influenced later jazz performers.

Cole had over 100 hits on the pop charts and was the first Black man to host a television series in America. He died of cancer at age 45. His daughter Natalie Cole, just 15 when her father passed away, became a famous singer. Using Nat's recorded voice, she sang a duet with him in 1991. The song "Unforgettable"— originally recorded by Cole in 1951—became a hit for the second time. In 1992, the album and the song won seven Grammy awards, including Best Album and Best Song.

Cole learned to play the organ from his mother, a church organist.

Inside the high school, Black students were segregated in the cafeteria. If Black students sat with white students, they were forced to move. When there was an assembly, there were two bells rung: one was for Black students to head up to the auditorium's balcony, and another for the rest of the students to gather below.

A Dangerous Position

Heading a chapter of the NAACP was risky. Not only was there a chance Burnett could be physically attacked, but his job security was also at risk. Employers often took a negative view of desegregation, and this kept many African Americans from joining the NAACP. Burnett often found himself speaking to an audience of only a few people at his meetings. But a few was better than none.

Burnett did not fear **retribution**. Nothing mattered more to him than ending segregation—not his job at the local veterans hospital,

Robert L. Carter assisted NAACP chief counsel Thurgood Marshall in many important civil rights cases.

not even his safety. He became a fixture at every Topeka Board of Education meeting from 1948 to1950, seated in the audience and making pointed remarks when it was time for public comments.

Over and over, he requested that the school board end elementary school segregation. Over and over, they refused. Finally, Burnett presented the school board with a petition for integration signed by 1,500 people. Surely this would show board members that they must give in to reason—people wanted change! But the board ignored the petition and told Burnett again: There would be no desegregation.

After two years of speaking at meetings with no sign of support from any of the board members, Burnett realized what he needed to do. It was time for legal action.

Unstoppable

Burnett suffered from **leukemia**, but he wouldn't let his disease stop him any more than he let fear. He set to work with the Topeka NAACP's legal team: attorneys Charles Bledsoe and John and Charles Scott. Bledsoe wrote to the National NAACP's legal department to advise them of the Topeka NAACP's plan to file a lawsuit against the school board and ask their advice. Assistant Special Counsel Robert L. Carter wrote back with suggestions on how to proceed.

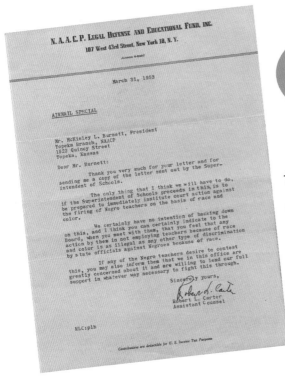

N.A.A.C.P. LEGAL DEFENSE AND EDUCATIONAL FUND, INC.
107 West 43rd Street, New York 18, N.Y.

March 31, 1953

AIRMAIL SPECIAL

Mr. McKinley L. Burnett, President
Topeka Branch, NAACP
1522 Quincy Street
Topeka, Kansas

Dear Mr. Burnett:

Thank you very much for your letter and for sending me a copy of the letter sent out by the Superintendent of Schools.

The only thing that I think we will have to do, if the Superintendent of Schools proceeds in this, is to be prepared to immediately institute court action against the firing of Negro teachers on the basis of race and color.

We certainly have no intention of backing down on this, and I think you can certainly indicate to the Board, when you meet with them, that you feel that any action by them in not employing teachers because of race and color is as illegal as any other type of discrimination by state officials against Negroes because of race.

If any of the Negro teachers desire to contest this, you may also inform them that we in this office are greatly concerned about it and are willing to lend our full support in whatever way necessary to fight this through.

Sincerely yours,

Robert L. Carter
Assistant Counsel

RLC:plh

Contributions are deductible for U. S. Income Tax Purposes

Carter's letter to the Topeka NAACP advising them about raising the funds necessary to appeal *Brown* to the Supreme Court.

Carter advised Bledsoe to find **plaintiffs** with elementary-age children from the lowest to the highest grades, so that even if the case stalled in court for years, there would always be a plaintiff whose child had been affected by segregation. He also told Bledsoe to argue that Topeka's segregation law was **unconstitutional**. This would entitle them to the opportunity to go straight to the U.S. Supreme Court.

Carter saw the potential for this case, especially because there had been desegregation success earlier in Kansas. The state of Kansas could be the key to overturning the *Plessy v. Ferguson* ruling that "separate but equal" schools were constitutional. He offered to work together with Bledsoe on a draft of the lawsuit.

Was Carter right about this opportunity? Bledsoe didn't know. His focus was to help the African American children in Topeka, Kansas. The rest of the country was too much to consider right now.

The First Recruit

Burnett, Bledsoe, and the Scotts set about their mission to recruit parents as plaintiffs. Lucinda Todd, the first volunteer, was more than willing—she was downright thrilled.

Todd had been a teacher until she got married and then was forced to quit her job because married women weren't allowed to teach. She joined the Topeka NAACP and was elected secretary in 1948. Todd was determined to publicly criticize the Topeka Board of Education. She met with Black school teachers in secret who had been threatened with termination if they spoke up against their **oppressive** work environment and the inequality in their schools. She had to pull her window shades down when the teachers came over because they were so scared they would be caught speaking with her.

From left to right: Alvin, Nancy, and Lucinda Todd.

Undaunted

In 1948, Todd knocked on the doors of Topeka's Black households, handing out leaflets to nearly every African American family. This paper informed them of the Citizens Committee on Civil Rights whose mission was to fight back against discrimination in schools. The flyer gave out her address and phone number—a very daring move. Unfortunately, most Black families were too intimidated to join.

A Mother's Outrage

As a parent, Todd was outraged at the discrepancies

Nancy Todd attended the segregated Buchanan Elementary School in Topeka. The children of six other *Brown* plaintiffs attended Buchanan too.

Death of Oscar Micheaux

Oscar Micheaux, a novelist and considered to be America's first major Black feature filmmaker, passed away on March 25, 1951.

Early on, Micheaux wanted to be his own boss. He opened a shoeshine stand, through which he learned about business and saved up money.

Establishing the Micheaux Film and Book Company, Micheaux became a major producer and director. U.S. and international audiences flocked to over 40 films he produced, which examined race relations in America. Micheaux wanted to portray Black people and their struggles in an honest way. His goal was to be authentic and true to himself and African American culture—and he succeeded.

Micheaux's gravestone is inscribed: "A man ahead of his time."

Oscar Micheaux's films and books shined an honest and harsh light on the struggles African Americans faced.

between Black and white schools. She wanted her daughter, Nancy Jane Todd, to have music lessons—but music was only taught at white schools. In 1950, she confronted the school board, who told her that Black children weren't interested in studying music

Oliver Brown (right) and his family faced a tough road ahead when he became the only male plaintiff challenging Topeka's segregated schools.

and their families couldn't afford the instruments. After Todd spoke out, music was offered in Black schools the following year.

One victory was wonderful. Now Todd wanted more equality, and not just for herself and Nancy. She wanted it for every Topeka family whose children were forced to ride on segregated buses away from their neighborhoods and local schools.

Finding a Father

Burnett's team used their network of friends to find more plaintiffs. The number grew, but one problem remained: These plaintiffs were all mothers.

They needed to find a father to sign on because the case would be taken more seriously by the courts if a man was involved. But men were busy with their jobs. And more than that, they were worried they would lose them.

Charles Scott approached a childhood friend. Oliver Brown had a young daughter named Linda Carol, and Scott knew Linda had a hard time traveling to school. Scott visited Brown and explained the lawsuit. But when Scott finished talking, Brown declined. ■

Linda Brown's harsh walk to her bus stop to attend the segregated Monroe Elementary prompted her father to reconsider participating in the Topeka lawsuit.

2

A Look Inside

In 1951, Oliver Brown's daughter was still attending a segregated school. But her father's position on becoming part of the NAACP lawsuit had changed. He'd grown tired of watching Linda, a third grader, endure brutal weather conditions walking six blocks to her school bus stop to ride to Monroe Elementary. Her segregated Black school was one mile away, while Sumner Elementary, a white school, was much closer to her house. Some winter days she couldn't make it to her bus stop because the cold became too much for her to bear. Her tears froze on her face.

While Brown certainly wanted better for his daughter, being an activist was not in his plans. A welder for a railroad, Brown was also studying to become a minister. Being a plaintiff in a court case was a dangerous choice. He knew well that Black people who took a stand were in jeopardy of loss of life, loss of work, having their homes and churches burned, and being run out of town.

What Was Right

Brown's wife convinced him that he needed to stand up for what was right and give a better life and education not only to their children, but to all Black children. This was especially true because he would soon be a minister. He felt it was his calling to help Black citizens rise up.

Linda (left) and her sister, Terry Lynn Brown, outside of Monroe Elementary School in Topeka.

Porgy and Bess

The first complete recording of George Gershwin's famous opera *Porgy and Bess* was recorded between April 5 and 13, 1951. The "folk opera" first debuted on stage in Boston on September 30, 1935. It then opened on Broadway in New York City on October 10, 1935.

Classically trained African American singers made up the cast, which was a bold and unusual choice for the time. Though the opera itself was controversial, its music was heralded, and it continues to be performed and recorded today. It is estimated that one of the songs— "Summertime"—has been recorded more than 25,000 times by various artists. The first person to have a hit with it on the charts was Billie Holiday. Other famous recordings were by Miles Davis, Louis Armstrong and Ella Fitzgerald, and Charlie Parker.

Urylee Leonardos as Bess and William Warfield as Porgy perform in the 1950s world tour of *Porgy and Bess*.

Maude Lawton was determined to make Topeka's schools integrated like its neighborhoods.

Lena Carper also wanted to spare her daughter Katherine from treacherous weather conditions walking to her school bus.

With Oliver Brown on board, the NAACP could employ the legal strategy they sought, using a man's name to headline the case.

More Plaintiffs

Burnett and his team recruited 13 parents with 20 children in total. Two of the plaintiffs were Maude Lawton and Lena Carper.

Lawton was an active member of the Lane Street Church of God, as was Burnett. With Burnett's and Charles Scott's encouragement, Lawton joined the lawsuit on behalf of her six-year-old daughter, Victoria Jean. Lawton was set on seeing

Victoria not have to walk so far to get to Buchanan Elementary School (for Black children) when a white school was a block away. It was puzzling to Victoria that she was at a segregated school while her neighborhood was integrated and everyone got along well.

Lena Carper's daughter, 10-year-old Katherine, was the oldest child involved in the case. Carper would walk Katherine to the bus stop every day. The dirt roads turned to mud when it rained. Even with rubber boots on, the Carpers frequently stopped to clean off their caked soles with a stick. But rain was nothing compared to the snow and brutal cold. Once they made it to the bus stop, there was no shelter. They stood outside in nature's harshest weather, praying the bus would be on time.

Ready

Each plaintiff was told to bring their child to the closest school for white children and try to enroll them. Once the enrollment was denied, they reported back to the Topeka NAACP. This gave Bledsoe and the Scotts the documentation to file *Oliver L. Brown et al. v. The Board of Education of Topeka*. Their day in court was coming, and they were ready for it.

Failure to Obey

President Harry S. Truman fired General of the Army Douglas MacArthur on April 11, 1951. NAACP attorney Thurgood Marshall blamed the persistent racism in the armed forces on MacArthur, who believed that white Americans were superior to African Americans. More than hurtful, this discrimination carried devastating consequences during the Korean War (1950–1953). Members of the 503rd Field Artillery Battalion, a Black artillery unit, were being held as prisoners of war. Because the Black battalion didn't receive as many supplies to fight as the other units, they'd lost a battle with tremendous casualties at the end of 1950 and were captured.

Once MacArthur was fired, the integration of the army happened rapidly. But it was too late for the 503rd Field Artillery Battalion. Many of the survivors were imprisoned for up to three years.

After being terminated, Douglas MacArthur gave a farewell speech to Congress on April 19, 1951.

A Second Suit

In the early winter, James Nabrit, Jr., a professor at Howard University School of Law, a historically Black college and university (HBCU), filed a lawsuit in the District of Columbia on behalf of Black students seeking admission to an all-white school.

Nabrit worked independently of the NAACP, but he shared their determination to attack the concept of "separate but equal" and have it ruled unconstitutional.

James Nabrit, Jr., later became the first African American to serve as Deputy U.S. Ambassador to the United Nations.

EQUAL FACILITIES for all Children

No Second Class Schools for First Class Pupils

WE WANT TO STUDY NOT WALK

Washington, DC, activist Gardner Bishop pickets with parents, protesting an inferior school for Black children.

Denied

Things came to a head in the District of Columbia when Gardner Bishop—a local barber, civil rights activist, and member of the Consolidated Parents Group—attempted to get 11 African American students admitted to the new, magnificent-looking John Philip Sousa Junior High School. The principal gave them a tour, and the students were in awe of its spacious and modern classrooms and multiple basketball courts. But the principal refused to enroll the students, even though there was plenty of room for them.

Officially denied enrollment, these students now had grounds for a lawsuit: *Bolling v. Sharpe*. The case's named plaintiff, 12-year-old Spottswood Bolling, was one of the students who visited the school and tried to enroll. However, all 11 students were included in the court case. Sharpe was C. Melvin Sharpe, president of the District of Columbia Board of Education.

"Separate but equal" was now twice challenged—one case in Topeka and one in the District of Columbia—and things were just heating up. ■

Built in 1950, John Philip Sousa Junior High School was modern, well-equipped, and off limits to Black students.

The outside of Robert Russa Moton High School in Virginia where Barbara Johns was a student.

3

A Teenage Crusader

Sixteen-year-old student Barbara Johns was frustrated with her all-Black high school in Prince Edward County, Virginia. Robert Russa Moton High School had no cafeteria, gymnasium, nurse, or teachers' restrooms. Not only were the available resources far worse than at the white school across town—but her school had double the students it had been designed to hold. Classes were even held in an old, rusted school bus outside because space inside the school was so limited. When parents asked the school board for a bigger and better-equipped building, the board ordered shacks for the overflow of students.

What Could a Student Do?

Johns couldn't imagine that the school board

wouldn't want to help students. Surely, they didn't understand the severity of the situation. But what could she—a student—do to show them when parents couldn't?

This was on her mind when she missed her school bus one morning—only to watch a bus for white students drive past her.

Bursting with unrest, Barbara spoke with a teacher she trusted. This teacher urged her to take action.

Johns met with a group of classmates to share a daring plan: She wanted to organize a student strike. She braced herself for their refusal—but they agreed to help.

Taking the Stage

On April 23, Johns's carefully constructed plan went into action. First, the school principal, M. Boyd Jones, left the building when he was falsely told some students had walked out of school and were causing trouble downtown.

By leading a strike against intolerable conditions, Barbara Johns led the way for future student civil rights activists.

Remembering Barbara Johns

Barbara Johns put her life in danger when she took her stand in 1951. The Ku Klux Klan burned a cross on her family's lawn, and Johns's little sister Joan feared the Klan would take Barbara away.

Johns's brave stance was overlooked at the time. Decades later in 1998, Robert Russa Moton High School was declared a National Historic Landmark, and it became the Robert Russa Moton Museum. Virginia artist Louis Briel painted a portrait of Johns for display in the museum.

In July 2008, the Virginia Civil Rights Memorial opened on Capitol Square in Richmond. Johns is represented by one of eight statues, with her words engraved in granite: "It seemed like reaching for the moon."

On the west side of the Virginia Civil Rights Memorial, Barbara Johns's statue reaches for what is right.

Fired after the walkout, R. R. Moton principal M. Boyd Jones was still proud of his students who "helped change the history of this nation."

Next, Johns **forged** a memo to the teachers from the principal, directing them to bring their classes to the auditorium for a special assembly. The teachers left their students there as instructed.

Johns took the stage. She addressed the 450 students, revealing her plans for a student strike to protest the unequal conditions of the Black and white schools. Again, she braced herself for rejection. After all, the students could face serious consequences if the strike failed. Certainly, she would, for instigating such a thing. She could be **expelled**.

Marching

To Johns's relief, the students all agreed to join her strike. They marched down to the county courthouse together. The students would make officials aware of the unacceptable conditions they faced, while the white students did not.

Johns and her fellow student leaders went inside School Superintendent T. J. McIlwaine's office. He scolded them: They were out of place! This took Johns aback. She had believed the strike would make county officials aware of their situation and sympathize with them. She had envisioned a new school being built. But instead, no one cared.

One of the signs Moton students carried during their strike.

Josephine Baker Day

Internationally known African American actress, singer, and dancer Josephine Baker was a leading force in the early civil rights movement, and the NAACP celebrated her activism by naming May 20, 1951, "Josephine Baker Day."

Born in St. Louis, Missouri, Baker achieved her fame in France. When she returned to America, she and her white husband encountered much racism, so she did something about it. She refused to perform in cities with segregated audiences—even turning down $10,000 from a Miami club. She called out discrimination in articles and lectures.

Baker had always felt comfortable in New York City—until October 16, 1951. That night, she was brought as

Members from the NAACP protest in front of the Stork Club on October 22, 1951.

a dinner guest to the Stork Club, an exclusive Manhattan nightclub. While her white hosts received their dinners, Josephine and her friend Bessie A. Buchanan, a Black woman, did not. After an hour of waiting for her steak and crab salad, Josephine went to a pay phone outside and called her lawyer, NAACP head Walter White. She also called the police and charged discrimination against the club.

Black and white New Yorkers picketed the Stork Club, and the story made the international news. Though criminal charges were dropped, the Stork Club's reputation and popularity suffered a major hit, and the establishment went into a permanent downslide, eventually closing.

Josephine Baker did not tolerate being discriminated against at the Stork Club.

It didn't take long for Johns to recover her grit. She led the students back to their school. They picketed for the rest of the day, inside and out, holding signs that declared, "We want a new school or none at all!"

NAACP Joins In

The students continued their strike the next day, and the day after that. Johns and her classmate Carrie Stokes reached out to the NAACP in Richmond, Virginia.

NAACP attorney Oliver Hill promised to meet with

them. Once he agreed that the NAACP would act on their behalf, the students returned to school on May 7. The strike had lasted 10 days.

Later that month, Hill's colleague Spottswood Robinson filed a suit in federal court on behalf of the students. Johns was not named as the plaintiff in the case. Randomly, a ninth-grade girl named Dorothy Davis was listed in *Dorothy E. Davis v. County School Board of Prince Edward County*. Barbara Johns didn't mind. She wasn't looking for fame—just a decent school to learn in. ■

Dorothy Davis stands center in a group of student plaintiffs in Prince Edward County, Virginia.

Thurgood Marshall argued 32 civil rights cases before the Supreme Court. He won 29 of them.

4

A Measure of How Far

Spottswood Robinson rushed from filing his court papers in Prince Edward County, Virginia, down to Charleston, South Carolina. He was due in federal court on May 28 as part of the legal team arguing for the plaintiff in *Briggs v. Elliott*, another challenge to a segregated school system.

A Simple Request

Briggs v. Elliott began as a request by Black parents in Summerton, a town in Clarendon County, South Carolina. Harry Briggs, a service station attendant, and Eliza Briggs, a maid, joined 21 other Black families to chip in for a secondhand school bus for their children, who had to walk up to 16 miles round trip to and from school each day. The children also had to gather wood for heaters inside their shabby educational facility. The bus kept breaking down, and the families could not afford its maintenance. They asked the school superintendent, Roderick W. Elliott, to provide a bus for their children. He declined, saying that the Black families didn't pay enough in taxes, and it wouldn't be fair to the white taxpayers.

Reverend Joseph DeLaine, a teacher at St. Paul Rural Primary School, one of the run-down Black schools, took up the cause for the parents at great risk to his job. He had heard a speech by Reverend James Hinton, president of the South Carolina NAACP, encouraging Black families to challenge the legality of educational discrimination. At first, he organized a letter-writing campaign to state officials, with no results. That's when he contacted the legal arm of the NAACP.

Thurgood Marshall

Thurgood Marshall was the lead attorney on *Briggs v. Elliott*. The 42-year-old chief counsel for the NAACP Legal Defense and Educational Fund had much experience and success in arguing civil rights cases, several of them before the Supreme Court. A descendant of enslaved people, Marshall was turned on to law by his father, who took Marshall and his brother to watch court cases as bystanders. He wanted to attend law

17-year-old Thurgood Marshall's high school graduation picture.

school in his hometown, Baltimore, at the University of Maryland School of Law, but their segregation policy kept him from applying. Instead, Marshall went to Howard University School of Law. His mother had to **pawn** her engagement and wedding rings to pay for his tuition. He started his law career in a private practice, but when he was invited to represent the NAACP in a law school discrimination case, he joined their staff.

Expectation of Loss

Marshall decided to change *Briggs* from an *equalization* case into a *desegregation* case. Instead of asking for enforcement of "separate but equal" by bringing the African American schools up to the standards of the white schools, the plaintiffs asked for school segregation to be declared unconstitutional.

He expected to lose in South Carolina—and he wanted to. That way, he could appeal the case to the Supreme Court.

Plaintiffs with their children in the Clarendon County school segregation case.

George Washington Carver National Monument

On June 14, 1951, 210 acres of the Moses Carver farm in Missouri—George Washington Carver's boyhood home—were turned over to the National Park Service to create the George Washington Carver National Monument. It was the first national monument dedicated to someone other than a president, and the first to be created for an African American.

Born into slavery, Carver was raised by his owner, Moses Carver, as a son. His thirst for knowledge led him to graduate from high school and head to college—not at all typical for a Black man at that time.

Carver became well known for his knowledge about crop rotation and restoring depleted soil while teaching, researching, and experimenting at Tuskegee Institute, a historically Black university in Tuskegee, Alabama. His research on new uses for peanuts, pecans, soybeans, sweet potatoes, and other crops brought him greater fame.

President Franklin D. Roosevelt dedicated $30,000 on July 14, 1943, for the George Washington Carver National Monument to be established. It took until 1951 for the land to be secured. Two years later, it was opened to the public.

A statue of Carver sits in front of the George Washington Carver National Monument.

Packed House

Black men and women started lining up outside the South Carolina courthouse at sunrise on May 28, the first day of the trial. More Black families kept arriving, many in caravans from all over the South. When the courtroom began to fill its 150 seats, the line to get in wove from the second-floor courtroom down the hall, down the front steps, and spilled out onto the sidewalks. Five hundred people stood outside in the intense southern summer heat, excited at this chance for Black Americans to be heard in court.

The crowd stood there for the entire day. Whenever Marshall or Robinson made an important

Harry Briggs (center) and some of the other plaintiffs in the *Briggs v. Elliott* case.

point, someone sitting in the courtroom would get up and whisper it to the line of people in the hall, and the news would travel down the line all the way to everyone outside.

Reverend James Hinton was deeply moved by the trial, observing that it was a measure of how far they—the NAACP and all Black Americans—had come. "The very sight of the trial lifted [Blacks] to deeper appreciation of the NAACP and its aims and purposes. The Blacks from Clarendon County and from all over the South jammed the courthouse, standing shoulder to shoulder, hot and uncomfortable, for a single purpose—to demonstrate to all the world that Blacks in the South are determined to eliminate segregation from American life."

Retaliation

As expected, the plaintiffs lost the case. The **injunction** to abolish segregation was denied, although their request to equalize educational facilities was granted. Julius Waring was one of the three judges, and the only one who voted for the plaintiffs.

Crosses were burned near Judge Waring's house and a brick was thrown through a window. Newspaper articles blasted Waring. Political and community leaders criticized and shunned him and his wife to the point that they left the state.

Medal of Honor

On August 6, 1951, William Henry Thompson of the 24th Infantry Regiment received the United States military's highest decoration, the Medal of Honor, for his bravery in the Korean War. He had been killed in action the year before, but after his death he became the first Black soldier to earn the Medal of Honor in the Korean conflict, and the first Black soldier to earn one since 1898.

Thompson's platoon had been ambushed by (North) Korean People's Army troops. Several men in the company fled when shots were fired. Thompson remained and soon came under heavy fire. He was shot several times but did not tell anyone. His commanding officer discovered his wounds and ordered him twice to withdraw with the rest of the troops, but Thompson kept firing.

No one could remove Thompson; he refused to leave and told his fellow soldiers, "Get out of here, I'll cover you!" As the platoon reluctantly retreated without Thompson, they heard grenades, and Thompson's gun fell silent. He had protected the other soldiers in his unit as they withdrew.

Medal of Honor recipient William Henry Thompson found comfort and purpose in military life after being homeless as a youth.

Judge Julius Waring and his wife, Elizabeth, at their home in Charleston, South Carolina.

Reverend DeLaine was fired from his teaching post. His wife, Mattie, was also fired from her job, as were all the other letter writers from the campaign. DeLaine's home and church were burned. He moved to Buffalo, New York, after surviving an attempted drive-by shooting. Both Harry and Eliza Briggs also lost their jobs.

Topeka Trial

On June 25, *Oliver L. Brown et al. v. The Board of Education of Topeka* went to trial in federal court. One by one, the plaintiffs testified that they had brought their children to be enrolled in white schools and were denied.

Five of the *Brown* plaintiffs with their children. Pictured are, front row, from left: students Vicki Henderson, Donald Henderson, Linda Brown, James Emanuel, Nancy Todd, and Katherine Carper; back row, from left, parents Zelma Henderson, Oliver Brown, Sadie Emanuel, Lucinda Todd, and Lena Carper.

Katherine Carper, the oldest of the plaintiffs' children, also testified. The courtroom was the largest room the 10-year-old had ever seen, and it was packed with people. And yet, she felt no fear. Her mother had told her that she would be asked some questions about her school by men who were lawyers, and that she should just tell the truth.

So, she did.

One of the things they asked her about was the bus ride, which was on a city bus, not a school bus. She talked about the ride home being scary, over-crowded with kids standing in the aisle getting bumped and thrown around. Fights would break out, but the white bus driver did nothing to stop it.

Understanding

After that day in court, Katherine did feel scared. Now she understood some of what was going on. She understood that her teachers' jobs were threatened, and she worried for them. Most of all, she felt bad for saying anything negative about her school. She didn't have any complaints about her teachers. They were wonderful! Katherine wondered if they would be mad at her now, but much to her relief, her teachers all treated her the same. ■

White rioters attack a Cicero, Illinois, apartment building after a Black family moved in, setting fire to the family's furniture.

5

A Long Journey

In July, Louis Redding, Delaware's first Black attorney, filed a lawsuit on behalf of eight African American parents. These parents were traveling 20 miles round trip to bring their children to Howard High School—the only high school for Black students in the entire state. Meanwhile, Claymont High School—a spacious and well-maintained all-white public school, was located in their town.

Distance was not the only factor. Their children were packed into overcrowded classrooms, their curriculum did not include all the lessons white children were taught, and some of the teachers' qualifications at Howard were questionable.

The parents consulted Redding, who advised them to ask state officials to admit their children into Claymont. When they were denied, Redding filed *Belton v. Gebhart*.

Ethel Louise Belton was one of the parents. Francis B. Gebhart was a member of the school board.

At the same time, Redding filed a similar case at the elementary school level: *Bulah v. Gebhart*.

Sarah Bulah was a parent who asked the state to provide bus transportation for her adopted Black daughter, Shirley Barbara, in Hockessin, a rural Delaware town. Particularly stinging was the fact that a bus for white children passed her house but would not stop for Shirley. The state officials' denial coldly pronounced that no bus transportation would be provided because Black children could not ride on a bus serving white children.

White Riot

In Cicero, Illinois (a Chicago suburb), Harvey E. Clark, Jr., an African American World War II veteran and graduate of Fisk University, rented an apartment in an all-white neighborhood. He and his family were initially stopped and threatened at gunpoint by police when they moved in, and the NAACP sued for Clark's right to live in that apartment.

At dusk on July 11, thousands of white people attacked the apartment building the Clark family lived in. The family members escaped to the rooftop before the rioting began, but the building was under siege. Rocks were thrown through windows, property was destroyed, and fires were started.

Sugar Ray Robinson

Boxer Sugar Ray Robinson won the World Middleweight title in 1951—twice. On February 14, he faced world middleweight champion Jake LaMotta in a fight for the title, knocking LaMotta out. The event became known as "The St. Valentine's Day Massacre."

Robinson set out for a series of European fights, driving his pink Cadillac around the continent. In London, on July 10, he unexpectedly lost his title to Randy Turpin. On September 12, he fought Turpin again to regain the championship. Ring Magazine named Robinson 1951's "Fighter of the Year."

Admired for his ability to fight in any style, Robinson stated that rhythm and instinct were the keys to winning. He has been called the greatest boxer of all time.

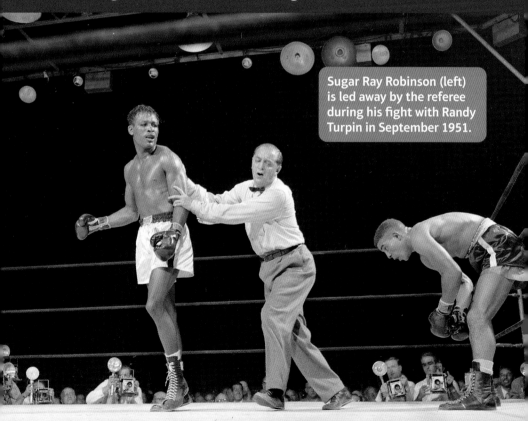

Sugar Ray Robinson (left) is led away by the referee during his fight with Randy Turpin in September 1951.

Harvey E. Clark, Jr., his wife, Johnetta, and their two children, Harvey III, six, and Michele, eight.

Sixty police officers could not control the mob, and firefighters were pelted with stones and bricks when they arrived on the scene. The police asked the firefighters to turn their hoses on the rioters, but the firefighters refused to do so without clearance from their lieutenant, who could not be reached.

As the world watched the horrific situation broadcast live on television, Illinois governor Adlai Stevenson sent in the Illinois National Guard. The rioters attacked the troops as well, and it would be days before they could end the riot, using weapons and tear gas. Most of the violence was over by July 14.

And $20,000 worth of damage had been done to the building (almost $210,000 in today's money).

Aftermath

None of the rioters were charged, but Clark's NAACP lawyer was **indicted** for starting a riot and **conspiracy** to damage property. Also indicted was the owner of the apartment building, the owner's rental agent, and the owner's lawyer. After much criticism, these charges were dropped.

The U.S. attorney general investigated, resulting in a grand jury indicting two Cicero officials and three police officers for violating Clark's civil rights.

Illinois National Guardsmen use bayonets to push back the swarming Cicero mob.

Duke Slater

The College Football Hall of Fame announced the first Hall of Fame Class on November 3, 1951. Frederick "Duke" Slater was the only African American to be inducted in its first year.

Slater played for the University of Iowa's Hawkeyes from 1918 to 1921. In that last year, the Hawkeyes were the national championship team, making him a First-Team All-American.

Slater became the first Black lineman in NFL history the following year. After his football career, he became a lawyer, practicing in Chicago, Illinois. In 1948, he was elected judge, receiving a million votes to be the second African American judge in Chicago history.

Twelve years later, he was elevated to the Cook County Superior Court, becoming the first African American appointed to Chicago's highest court.

Slater was inducted into the Pro Football Hall of Fame in 2020.

Frederick "Duke" Slater broke down racial barriers in sports and in politics.

Federal action in a civil rights housing case was rare because these cases were not given a priority.

Topeka Ruling

On August 3, the three-judge district court panel in Topeka ruled for the board of education in the *Brown* case. The judges found that segregation had a harmful effect on Black children, but they denied any changes since the educational system in Topeka was equal for both Black and white students. They cited the *Plessy v. Ferguson* precedent the Supreme Court had set in 1896—"separate but equal" was the rule unless the Supreme Court overturned it.

That is exactly what the NAACP aimed to do, but it would take years before they achieved their goal. ■

Johnny Bright, Drake University football player, was targeted for attack by an opposing Oklahoma team because of his race.

6

More Injustice

The final three months of 1951 would see an increase in Black student activism. But African Americans would also experience escalating violence against them—some of it deadly.

Stillwater, Oklahoma, became the scene of a violent racist attack on October 20. Johnny Bright was an African American college football player for the Drake University Bulldogs in Des Moines, Iowa. They were playing Oklahoma A&M College (now Oklahoma State University) at Oklahoma A&M's Lewis Field.

The Oklahoma team targeted Bright before the game. Many people witnessed team members calling Bright a racial slur and threatening that Bright would not be around at the end of the game.

Bright was knocked unconscious three times by the same opposing player during the first seven minutes of the game. The last blow broke his jaw and he had to leave the game shortly after.

Photographers captured the blows in six sequences, clearly displaying that the jaw-breaking blow came after Bright had handed the ball off to a teammate. The Oklahoma team maintained the attack was not intentional, even after confronted with the evidence. The college maintained a "no comment policy" for over half a century, until September 28, 2005. Twenty-two years after Johnny Bright's death, Oklahoma State University president David J. Schmidly wrote a letter to Drake president David Maxwell formally apologizing for the Johnny Bright Incident.

How Much More?

In Kinston, North Carolina, the students of all-Black Adkin High School valued their education—but they wondered how much more they could learn if they had the same materials and textbooks as the white students at Kinston's nearby Granger High School. Things were separate, but certainly not equal.

Segregated Adkin High School in Kinston, North Carolina.

Janet Collins

Prima ballerina Janet Collins broke the color barrier at New York's Metropolitan Opera on November 13, 1951. Performing in Giuseppe Verdi's *Aida*, she became the first Black artist to join the company's roster.

Collins had faced brutal discrimination in the dance world all her life. She could not take dance lessons with white children. As years went on, dance companies refused to hire her despite her ability.

Collins turned to performing in theaters. She became a Broadway sensation in New York City, winning an award for her first role. That's when she drew the attention of the Metropolitan Opera.

Although Collins was treated with equality by the Met, she was disheartened by the continued racism and discrimination she experienced while touring the country. Sometimes she stayed behind and let under-studies perform her role. She left the Met after three years.

Janet Collins rehearsing in 1955.

The Adkin students always tried to make the best of things, and they were a proud and vibrant student body. The marching band often paraded down local streets. The football team won championships.

That's why, out of everything they didn't have—a cafeteria, a library, microscopes and other learning tools, up-to-date textbooks—they wanted one thing above all: a gym.

The Last Straw

In November 1951, Adkin students heard that the

Adkin students had heard of a student strike in Virginia when they carefully planned their walkout.

Granger students were going to get a new gym built. This was too much to bear. They knew that workers went on strike to get what they deserved. The Adkin students decided to go on strike for their gym.

The students knew they couldn't risk telling any adults. Their parents had working relationships with white people in the community, which could be jeopardized. Their teachers could certainly get fired. So, the students created a code to listen for during the morning announcements.

"We Charge Genocide"

Another group that fought to end injustices against Black Americans was the Civil Rights Congress (CRC). Formed in 1946, it was a defense organization that was not supported by the United States government.

On December 17, 1951, the CRC delivered a petition entitled "We Charge **Genocide**: The Crime of Government Against the Negro People" to the United Nations in New York and to the United Nations assembly in Paris.

The 237-page document cited violent acts committed against Black Americans since 1945. It presents evidence demonstrating how Black Americans had been subjected to mistreatment and violence. It maintained that the United States government was guilty of the genocide of African Americans in its own country.

"We Charge Genocide" became known around the world. It was largely ignored by the mainstream press in the United States, and the U.S. State Department asked the NAACP to issue a statement rejecting it. The NAACP refused.

Activist Paul Robeson presents the United Nations with a copy of "We Charge Genocide."

On November 18, "Carolyn Caulfield has lost her little red pocketbook" came over the loudspeaker. That signaled the 700 members of the high school student body to walk out. The sounds of scraping chairs and scuffling feet resonated through the halls. The older students shepherded the younger ones into the center of the crowd.

The students walked peacefully downtown, some wearing signs stating why they were protesting. People stared at them but said nothing. They remained peaceful, respectful, and obeyed all pedestrian laws. They gathered at Carver Theater, the theater designated for the Black community.

Four days later, when the students returned to school after the Thanksgiving break, they were met with news: The school board had agreed to give them their gym.

No Hope

On a hot November day in 1951 in central Florida, longtime friends and veterans of World War II Walter Irvin and Samuel Shepherd, both 24, rode in the back seat of a squad car. The car was being driven by Lake County sheriff Willis V. McCall. Driving down a desolate dirt road, the cruiser's tires spewed dust. Handcuffed together, Irvin and Shepherd nevertheless possessed a hope they had not felt in the two years they'd spent in jail.

Wrongfully convicted of assaulting a white woman in Groveland, Florida, these two African American men had been sentenced to death. But Harry T. Moore, executive director of the Florida NAACP, had raised an uproar in the media about this injustice, and Thurgood Marshall had persuaded the Supreme Court to overturn their convictions and grant them a new trial. They were being transported from Raiford State Prison in Union County to Tavares, a city in Lake County, for this trial. For once, they could see past the horror they'd experienced since their arrests.

The car slowed. Then it stopped. Sheriff McCall got out and ordered both men out of the car. At close

Also in Groveland, Florida, three Black men were arrested and tortured until they signed confessions for a crime they did not commit.

range, McCall fired his gun at Irvin and Shepherd. Three bullets into Shepherd, two into Irvin.

Moore Demands Justice

Moore called for the sheriff's immediate suspension. McCall claimed that the prisoners had attempted to attack him, but Irvin had survived to tell the true story. He'd played dead next to his friend's lifeless body. He'd even survived a third wound, delivered when a deputy arrived, noticed Irvin was still breathing, and put a bullet in his neck.

End Injustice

Harry Moore's mission was to stop injustices to Black Americans like those inflicted upon Irvin and Shepherd. He and his wife, Harriette, both educators, founded the Brevard County, Florida, chapter of the NAACP in 1934 after

Lake County sheriff Willis V. McCall ruthlessly shot Walter Irvin and Samuel Shepherd, who were falsely accused of assault.

their two daughters were born. He would eventually start more than 70 NAACP Florida chapters. Moore was named state secretary for the Florida chapter of the NAACP, and later its president. He investigated every lynching in the state, urging Florida's federal government representatives again and again to work on passing a federal law against lynching and mob violence. He sued over Black voter registration barriers and campaigned for Black teachers to have

Harry and Harriette Moore in a family photo circa 1931 with Evangeline (in Harriette's arms) and Annie Rosalea.

the same pay as white teachers even though schools were segregated.

Moore also headed the Progressive Voters League. Through this organization, he raised the Florida Black voter registration to 31 percent of those eligible to vote—the highest percentage in all the southern states at the time.

Because of their activism, the Moores were fired from their teaching jobs. Harry became a paid employee of the NAACP.

Assassination

On December 25, 1951, six weeks after Harry Moore called for the suspension and arrest of McCall, he and Harriette celebrated their 25th wedding anniversary and Christmas in their Mims, Florida, home. Their 23-year-old daughter, Annie Rosalea, or "Peaches," was home with them. Evangeline, their 21-year-old daughter, was scheduled to return home for the holidays on December 27.

When the Moores went to sleep, they did not know about the bomb under their floorboards. Made of dynamite, it had been positioned directly under their bed.

Shortly after 10 p.m., someone lit the fuse to the bomb. The explosion was so loud that people heard it for miles. The outside of the house was ripped apart. Inside, the Moores' bed fell into the huge hole that had been their floor. Wooden beams collapsed from the ceiling.

Peaches' bed was covered in glass shards, but she was not injured. Her parents were both still alive. But the nearby hospital would not treat Black people. Harry Moore died in the ambulance on the 30-mile drive to the closest hospital for African Americans.

Harriette survived for nine days before she died in that hospital.

Evangeline stepped off the train on the 27th, expecting to see her parents waiting for her. Her uncle broke the devastating news, which she never got over. She would spend the rest of her life seeking justice for the murder of her parents. ∎

The Moores' home after a bomb planted under the master bedroom floor exploded, killing them.

Evangeline Moore never found closure for the murders of her parents, Harry and Harriette Moore.

The Legacy of 1951 in Civil Rights History

The assassination of Harry and Harriette Moore triggered nationwide protests, rallies, memorials, and other events following the news of the bombing. President Harry S. Truman and Florida governor Fuller Warren were flooded with **telegrams** and letters protesting the murders.

Jackie Robinson, the first African American to play major league baseball, held a memorial service for the Moores in New York City on January 5, 1952. Approximately 3,000 mourners attended.

The NAACP later held a memorial service in March 1952, in Madison Square Garden, New York City. This memorial was attended by 15,000 mourners. Speakers like poet and activist Langston Hughes paid their respects.

The State of Florida called the FBI to head the investigation of the Moores' murders, but the case was never solved, and no one was ever **prosecuted**.

The FBI was convinced that the Ku Klux Klan had committed the bombing and identified several local Klansmen as suspects but was never able to find enough evidence to bring charges.

Sheriff McCall was never indicted or suspended for murdering Shepherd and attempting to murder Irvin. There was a **hearing**, but the all-white jury was composed of McCall's friends and, within a half

hour, decided McCall was justified and acted in self-defense.

Irvin was retried after he recovered from his injuries. Despite a vigorous defense by Thurgood Marshall, he was again convicted and sentenced to death—but that sentence was changed in 1955 to life in prison by Florida governor LeRoy Collins.

Paroled in January 1968, Irvin was found dead in

Thurgood Marshall (right) and his NAACP legal team could not secure justice for Walter Lee Irvin at his second trial. Irvin (third from left) was found guilty again.

George E. C. Hayes, (left), Thurgood Marshall (center), and James M. Nabrit, Jr., are jubilant outside the U.S. Supreme Court in 1954.

his car the following year while visiting Lake County. While his death was officially ruled as occurring by natural causes, Marshall had his doubts. Irvin has a military gravestone in Groveland, Florida.

The city of Groveland and Lake County each apologized in 2016 to survivors of Irvin and Shepherd for the injustice committed against them. On April 18, 2017, both men were cleared of the crime by a vote of the Florida House of Representatives. The Florida Senate also passed a **resolution**. On January 11, 2019, the Florida Board of Executive Clemency voted to pardon the men, which Governor Ron DeSantis approved.

The five 1951 cases challenging school segregation—*Brown v. The Board of Education of Topeka, Bolling v. Sharpe, Davis v. County School Board of Prince Edward County, Briggs v. Elliott*, and *Belton v. Gebhart* (which had been combined with *Bulah v. Gebhart*)—would rise to the U.S. Supreme Court, thanks to the NAACP's Thurgood Marshall and James Nabrit, Jr. The Court would combine them into one landmark case in 1954 and overturn *Plessy v. Ferguson*'s "separate but equal" ruling once and for all.

The years ahead would see the Black community strengthening its resolve to achieve equality. Change was in the air. It would be a hard and dangerous road, but it was coming. ◼

Maya Angelou

Maya Angelou was a treasured, award-winning African American poet, author, and civil rights activist. Born Marguerite Annie Johnson on April 4, 1928, she was nicknamed Maya by her brother Bailey Jr., who called her "Mya (my) sister." After their parents divorced, their father put three-year-old Maya and four-year-old Bailey on a train alone, traveling from their home in St. Louis, Missouri, to Stamps, Arkansas, to live with their grandmother.

Esteemed poet, author, and performer Maya Angelou in her Harlem, New York, home in 2006.

A traumatic event in eight-year-old Maya's life caused her to become mute for nearly five years, not uttering one word. During that time, she developed her love of poetry and books. Bertha Flowers, a teacher and friend of the family, encouraged Maya to speak again, telling her that she could not truly love poetry until she spoke it.

Maya and Bailey eventually moved to Oakland, California, with their mother. After attending a trade school, Maya became San Francisco's first Black female streetcar conductor at age 16. A year later, she gave birth to a son, Clyde.

Angelou's *I know Why the Caged Bird Sings* was one of the first memoirs by an African American to reach a widespread audience.

At age 23, Maya married a white man named Tosh Angelos, even though interracial relationships were met with public hostility at the time. When Maya's marriage ended in 1954, she sang and danced at San Francisco nightclubs, changing her professional name from Marguerite—or Rita— Johnson to Maya Angelou. She set off for Europe to perform in a traveling production of the opera *Porgy and Bess*,

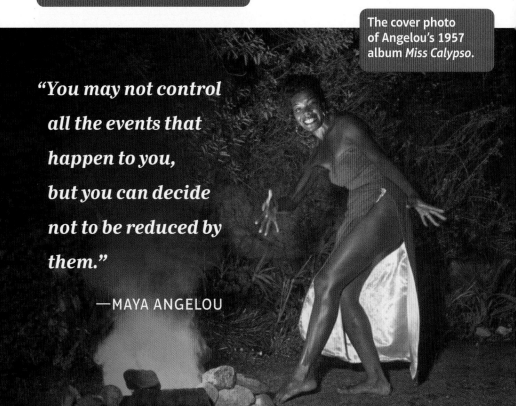

The cover photo of Angelou's 1957 album *Miss Calypso*.

"You may not control all the events that happen to you, but you can decide not to be reduced by them."

—MAYA ANGELOU

degrees. In 1981, she was given the lifetime Reynolds Professorship of American Studies at Wake Forest University in Winston-Salem, North Carolina. She became a full-time professor, teaching classes until 2011.

Angelou recited her poem "On the Pulse of Morning" at the 1993 presidential inauguration of Bill Clinton. President Clinton awarded her the National Medal of Arts in 2000. President Barack Obama awarded Angelou the Presidential Medal of Freedom in 2010. It is the highest civilian honor in the United States.

Maya Angelou passed away on May 18, 2014, at the age of 86. ■

A political activist, Angelou addresses the Democratic National Convention in 2004.

TIMELINE

The Year in Civil Rights

1951

FEBRUARY 28

Three NAACP lawyers filed a federal lawsuit on behalf of thirteen Topeka, Kansas, Black parents.

MARCH 25

Oscar Micheaux, a novelist, and America's first major Black feature filmmaker, passes away.

APRIL 23

Barbara Johns leads a student strike at Robert Russa Moton High School in Virginia.

MAY 28

The *Briggs v. Elliott* Supreme Court case begins.

JUNE 25

Oliver L. Brown et al. v. The Board of Education of Topeka goes to trial in federal court.

JULY 11

Thousands of white people attack an apartment building in Cicero, Illinois, after a Black family moves in.

AUGUST 6

William Henry Thompson of the 24th Infantry Regiment receives the United States military's highest decoration, the Medal of Honor.

SEPTEMBER 12

Sugar Ray Robinson beats Randy Turpin to win back the World Middleweight title.

OCTOBER 20

Johnny Bright, Drake University football player, is targeted for attack by an opposing Oklahoma team because of his race.

NOVEMBER 18

In Kinston, North Carolina, 700 students at the all-Black Adkin High School walk out in protest.

DECEMBER 17

The CRC delivers a petition entitled "We Charge Genocide: The Crime of Government Against the Negro People" to the United Nations in New York and to the United Nations assembly in Paris.

DECEMBER 25

Harry and Harriette Moore are killed in their home by a bomb planted under their bedroom.

GLOSSARY

activist (AK-tuh-vist) a person who works to bring about political or social change

amendment (uh-MEND-muhnt) a change that is made to a law or legal document

citizenship (SIT-i-zuhn-ship) the legal status of being a citizen of a country, with full rights to live, work, and vote there

civil rights (SIV-uhl rites) the individual rights that all members of a democratic society have to freedom and equal treatment under the law

conspiracy (kuhn-SPIR-uh-see) a secret plan made by two or more people to do something illegal or harmful

desegregation (dee-seg-ruh-GAY-shuhn) doing away with the practice of separating people of different races in schools, restaurants, and other public places

discrimination (dis-krim-uh-NAY-shuhn) prejudice or unfair behavior to others based on differences such as race, gender, or age

expelled (ik-SPELD) to make someone leave a school or organization, usually because of poor behavior

federal (FED-ur-uhl) national government, as opposed to state or local government

forged (forjd) to falsify a copy of something, such as money or a person's signature

genocide (JEN-uh-side) the deliberate and systematic destruction of a racial, political, or cultural group

hearing (HEER-ing) an opportunity for an accused person in a court case to tell their version of what happened

indict (in-DITE) to officially charge someone with a crime

injunction (in-JUNK-shuhn) a warning or order given by an authority

integration (in-ti-GRAY-shuhn) the act or practice of making facilities or an organization open to people of all races and ethnic groups

Jim Crow (jim kro) the practice of segregating Black people in the United States, named after a character who degraded African American life and culture

Ku Klux Klan (KOO kluks KLAN) a secret organization in the United States that uses threats and violence to achieve its goal of white supremacy; also called the Klan or the KKK

leukemia (loo-KEE-mee-uh) a serious disease of the bone marrow, which produces too many white blood cells

lynching (LIN-ching) a sometimes public murder by a group of people, often involving hanging

oppressive (uh-PRES-iv) to use power or authority in a cruel or unfair way

pawn (pawn) to leave a valuable item with a pawnbroker in return for money

plaintiff (PLAYN-tif) a person who brings a legal action

prosecute (PRAH-si-kyoot) to begin and carry out legal action in a court of law against a person accused of a crime

resolution (rez-uh-LOO-shuhn) a formal expression of opinion, will, or intent voted by an official body or assembled group

retribution (re-truh-BYOO-shuhn) the dispensing of punishment

segregation (seg-ruh-GAY-shuhn) the act or practice of keeping people or groups apart

telegram (TEL-uh-gram) a message sent by a system that uses a code of electrical signals sent by wire or radio

unconstitutional (un-kahn-stuh-TOO-shuhn-uhl) not in keeping with the basic principles or laws set forth in the U.S. Constitution

BIBLIOGRAPHY

Booth, Lance. "Overlooked No More: Barbara Johns, Who Defied Segregation in Schools." *The New York Times*, May 8, 2019.

Brown Henderson, Cheryl, Darren Canady, Deborah Dandridge, John Edgar Tidwell, and Vincent Omni. *Recovering Untold Stories: An Enduring Legacy of the Brown v. Board of Education Decision*. Kansas: University of Kansas Libraries, 2018.

Celotto, Bryce. "Bolling v. Sharpe and Beyond: The Unfinished and Untold History of School Desegregation in Washington, D.C." University of Massachusetts Thesis, 2016.

Moffson, Steven. "Equalization Schools in Georgia's African-American Communities, 1951-1970." Georgia Department of Natural Resources, Historic Preservation Division, 2010.

Thomas-Lester, Avis. "At Christmas, Evangeline Moore thinks of her martyred parents and demands justice." *The Washington Post*, December 25, 2011.

74 Million, the74million.org

Boundary Stones, boundarystones.weta.org

Brown Foundation for Educational Equity, Excellence and Research, brownvboard.org

C-Span, c-span.org

Kansas Historical Society, Lucinda Wilson Todd Collection, kshs.org

Library of Congress, loc.gov

Library of Virginia, lva.virginia.gov

Robert Russa Moton Museum, motonmuseum.org

Smithsonian, americanhistory.si.edu

South Carolina's Equalization
   Schools, scequalizationschools.org

Washington Area Spark,
   washingtonareaspark.com

Some of the *Brown* students from left to right: Vicki Henderson, Donald Henderson, Linda Brown, James Emanuel, Nancy Todd, and Katherine Carper.

INDEX

Adkin High School (Kinston, NC), 64, *64*, 66–67, *66–67*
Angelou, Maya, 82, *82*, 83, *83*, 84, *84*, 85, *85*, 86, 87, *86–87*

Baker, Josephine, 38–39, *39*
Belton, Ethel Louise, 55
Belton v. Gebhart, 55, 81
  Bishop, Gardner, 30, *30*
Bledsoe, Charles, 15–17
Bolling, Spottswood, 31
Bolling v. Sharpe, 31, 81
Briggs, Eliza, 43, 51
Briggs, Harry, 43, *48*, 51
Briggs v. Elliott, 43–44, 46, *48*, 81
Bright, Johnny, *62*, 63–64
Brown, Linda Carol, *8*, 21, *22*, 23, *24*, *52*
Brown, Oliver, *20*, 21, 23–24, *52*
Brown, Terry Lynn, *24*
Brown v. Board of Education, 11, 27, 51, 61, 81
Bulah, Sarah, 56
Bulah, Shirley Barbara, 56
Bulah v. Gebhart, 56
Burnett, McKinley, 11, *11*, 12, 14–15, 17, 21, 26

Caldwell, Harrison, 12
Carper, Katherine, 27, *52*, 53
Carper, Lena, 26, *26*, 27, *52*
Carter, Robert L., *14*, 15–16, *16*
Carver, George Washington, 47, *47*
Civil Rights Congress (CRC), 68
Clark, Harvey E., III, *58*
Clark, Harvey E., Jr., 56, *58*, 59
Clark, Johnetta, *58*
Clark, Michele, *58*
Cole, Nat King, 13, *13*
Cole, Natalie, 13
Collins, Janet, 65, *65*
Collins, LeRoy, 79

Davis, Dorothy, 41, *41*
Davis v. County School Board, 41, 81
DeLaine, Joseph, 44, 51
DeLaine, Mattie, 51

desegregation, 11, 14–16, 46
Elliott, Roderick W., 44
Emanuel, James, *52*
Emanuel, Sadie, *52*

Flowers, Bertha, 83

Gebhart, Francis B., 55
Groveland (FL), 70, *70*, 81

Hayes, George E. C., *80*
Henderson, Donald, *52*
Henderson, Vicki, *52*
Henderson, Zelma, *52*
Hill, Oliver, 40–41
Hinton, James, 44, 49
Hughes, Langston, 77

Irvin, Walter, 69–71, *71*, 78, *79*, 81

Jim Crow laws, 4, 5–6
John Philip Sousa Junior High School, 30, *31*
Johns, Barbara, 7, 33–34, *34*, 35, *35*, 36–37, 40–41
Johnson, Bailey, Jr., 82–83
Johnson, Clyde, 84
Jones, M. Boyd, 34, *36*

Kansas
  antislavery in, 10, *10*, 11
  desegregation lawsuits, 11–12, 14–17, *20*, 23, 26–27
  school segregation in, *8*, 9–10, 12, 14–16
Killens, John Oliver, 85
King, Martin Luther, Jr., 85
Ku Klux Klan (KKK), 6, 35, 78

Lawton, Maude, 26, *26*
Lawton, Victoria Jean, 26–27
Leonardos, Urylee, *25*

MacArthur, Douglas, 28, *28*
Marshall, Thurgood, *45*
  and the NAACP, *14*, 28, 44–46, 48
  and the Supreme Court, *42*, 70, *80*, 81
  and Walter Irvin, *79*, 81
McCall, Willis V., 69–71, *71*, 73, 78–79

McFarland, Kenneth, 12, *12*
Micheaux, Oscar, 19, *19*
Moore, Annie Rosalea, *72*, 73–74
Moore, Evangeline, *72*, 73, 75, *76*
Moore, Harriette, 7, *7*, 71, *72*, 73–75, *76*, 77
Moore, Harry T., 7, *7*, 70, 72, *72*, 73–74, *76*, 77

Nabrit, James, Jr., 29, *29*, *80*, 81
National Association for the
  Advancement of Colored People
  (NAACP)
  civil rights housing lawsuits, 56, 59, 61
  desegregation lawsuits, 6–7, 9–12,
    14–16, *16*, 17, *20*, 23, 27, 44, 48–49
  Stork Club protest, *38*, 39
  and student strikes, 40–41
National Association of Colored
  Women's Clubs (NACWC), 6

Plessy v. Ferguson, 6, 16, 61, 81
Porgy and Bess (opera), 25, *25*, 84

Redding, Louis, 55–56
Robert Russa Moton High School, *32*, 33, 35
Robeson, Paul, *68*
Robinson, Jackie, 77
Robinson, Spottswood, 41, 43, 48
Robinson, Sugar Ray, 57, *57*

School segregation
  busing to Black schools, 9–10, 21, *22*, 23, *26*, 27, 43–44, 53, 55–56
  parent plaintiffs in lawsuits, 16–17, *17*, *18*, *20*, 21, 23, 26, *26*, 27, 46, *52*
  student strikes, 7, 34, 36, *36*, 37, *37*, 40, *66*, 67, *67*, 69
  and unequal resources, *8*, 9–10, 17–18, 20–21, 30, *30*, 33–34, 36–37, 64, 66–67
Scott, Charles, 15, 17, 21, 26
Scott, John, 15, 17
"separate but equal" policy, 5–6, 10, 16, 29, 31, 46, 61, 81
Shepherd, Samuel, 69–71, *71*, 78, 81

Slater, Frederick "Duke," 60, *60*
Southern Christian Leadership
  Conference (SCLC), 85
Stokes, Carrie, 40
Stork Club (New York City), *38*, 39, *39*
Supreme Court, 6, 16, 44, 46, 61, *80*, 81

Thompson, William Henry, 50, *50*
Todd, Alvin, *17*
Todd, Lucinda, 17, *17*, 18, 20–21, *52*
Todd, Nancy, *17*, *18*, 20–21, *52*
Truman, Harry S., 28, 77

Warfield, William, *25*
Waring, Elizabeth, *51*
Waring, Julius, 49, *51*
"We Charge Genocide" petition, 68, *68*
white violence
  assassination of Black activists, 73–74, *74*, 75, *75–76*, 77–78
  against Black football players, *62*, 63–64
  against Black residents, *54*, 56, 58–59, *59*
  by police, 70–71
  retaliation against activists, 36, 51, 73

X, Malcolm, 85

About the Author

Selene Castrovilla is an acclaimed, award-winning author. Her five books on the American Revolution for young readers include Scholastic's *The Founding Mothers*. Selene has been a meticulous researcher of American history since 2003. She has expanded her exploration into the civil rights movement, as well as the Civil War, in a forthcoming book. A frequent speaker about our nation's evolution, she is equally comfortable with audiences of children and adults. Please visit selenecastrovilla.com.

PHOTO CREDITS

Photos ©: cover, 1: Allsport/Hulton Archive/Getty Images; 3 top: Carl Iwasaki/Getty Images; 3 bottom: Alfred Eisenstaedt/The LIFE Picture Collection/Shutterstock; 4: Everett Collection Inc/Alamy Images; 7: The Washington Post/Getty Images; 8: Carl Iwasaki/Getty Images; 10: Classic Image/Alamy Images; 11: Library of Congress; 12: Denver Post/Getty Images; 13: Michael Ochs Archives/Getty Images; 14: The Granger Collection; 16, 17, 18: Kansas Historical Society; 19: Science Source; 20, 22, 24: Carl Iwasaki/Getty Images; 25: Lebrecht Music Arts/Bridgeman Images; 28: Fotosearch/Getty Images; 29: Alfred Eisenstaedt/The LIFE Picture Collection/Shutterstock; 30: Washington Area Spark/Flickr; 31: John Philip Sousa Junior High School/https://historicsites.dcpreservation.org/items/show/564; 32: the Richmond Times-Dispatch/Encyclopedia Virginia; 34: Courtesy of Joan Johns Cobbs; 35: Frank Tozier/Alamy Images; 36: MotonSchoolHistory.org; 37: the Richmond Times-Dispatch/Encyclopedia Virginia; 38: Marty Lederhandler/AP Images; 39: Everett/Shutterstock; 40–41: Hank Walker/The LIFE Picture Collection/Shutterstock; 42: Everett/Shutterstock; 45: Courtesy of Supreme Court Historical Society; 46: University of South Carolina/South Caroliniana Library; 47: Shutterstock; 48: University of South Carolina/South Caroliniana Library; 50: U.S. Army/Wikimedia; 51: AP Images; 52: Carl Iwasaki/Getty Images; 54: AP Images; 57: Walter Kelleher/NY Daily News Archive/Getty Images; 58: John Lent/AP Images; 59: AP Images; 60: Chicago Sun-Times/AP Images; 62: Drake University Archives & Special Collections; 64: Courtesy of State Archives of North Carolina; 65: Sam Falk/New York Times Co/Getty Images; 68: Courtesy of People's World; 70: Everett/Shutterstock; 71: Wallace Kirkland/The LIFE Picture Collection/Shutterstock; 72: The Washington Post/Getty Images; 74–75: State Archives of Florida; 76: Patrick Semansky/AP Images; 78–79: Bettmann/Getty Images; 80: AP Images; 82–83: Chester Higgins Jr/The New York Times/Redux; 84 top: AP Images; 84 bottom: Gene Lester/Getty Images; 85: David Brewster/Star Tribune/Getty Images; 86–87: Timothy A. Clary/AFP/Getty Images; 88 top left: Carl Iwasaki/Getty Images; 88 top right: Courtesy of Joan Johns Cobbs; 88 center left: Walter Kelleher/NY Daily News Archive/Getty Images; 88 top center right: University of South Carolina/South Caroliniana Library; 88 bottom center right: Carl Iwasaki/Getty Images; 88 bottom left: Science Source; 88 bottom right: AP Images; 89 top left: U.S. Army/Wikimedia; 89 center left: Walter Kelleher/NY Daily News Archive/Getty Images; 89 center right: Courtesy of People's World; 89 bottom left: Drake University Archives & Special Collections; 89 bottom right: The Washington Post/Getty Images; 93: Carl Iwasaki/Getty Images.